A

CULTURE

OF

LEADERSHIP

Lessons Learned and Shared

DON SIPES, LFACHE

A Culture of Leadership--Lessons Learned and Shared

©2020, Don Sipes

ISBN: 978-1-09834-463-4

ISBN eBook: 978-1-09834-464-1

TABLE OF CONTENTS

BIOGRAPHY

From a vantage point of fifty years of engagement in the field of healthcare, Don Sipes began to explore thoughts he had developed about transitioning to a new era in his life—retirement. When he reached traditional retirement age, he decided to defer stepping away from his career for a period of time while he contemplated what activities were most important to make the next era of his next life meaningful. His introspection during this time brought him to the conclusion that his new mission needed to include sharing with current and emerging leaders the perspectives that he had accumulated through associations with other leaders, as well as experiences—both rewarding and painful—that shaped his career as a leader. These would be shared in the hope that such sharing could be a resource as these leaders faced their own often-daunting challenges.

Don's career path started with immersion in nearly all of the clinical aspects of healthcare delivery. Academically, he completed formal training in medical technology after earning his undergraduate degree in zoology (pre-medicine) from the University of Missouri–Columbia, followed by completion of a graduate degree in healthcare management from the University of Central Michigan. This training and experience formed the foundation of his leadership style as his professional calling transitioned from clinical to management. Although his initial healthcare posts were in smaller community settings, the opportunities he encountered over the years led to his serving as chair of the Missouri Hospital Association (MHA) and as regent for Missouri in the American College of Healthcare Executives (ACHE), being appointed to the American Hospital Association Regional Policy Board, and serving for more than twenty years as vice president of regional services for Saint Luke's Health System in Kansas City. He is the recipient of the MHA's highest honor, the Distinguished Service Award, as well as awards from ACHE and North Central Missouri College. He had the honor of directly sharing policy views with a U.S. president, a speaker of the U.S. House of Representatives, numerous senators and congressmen, and national and state healthcare leaders in more than thirty years of healthcare advocacy work in Washington, DC, and two state capitals. In his current phase of life, he continues to perform executive and professional coaching, to assist with curriculum development and education in higher-education settings, and to fulfill a commitment he made to himself to share his thoughts in written form with aspiring and practicing leaders.

Don resides in Kansas City, Missouri, with his wife, Linda. Their family includes two children and two grandchildren.

PREFACE

As I write this book, our world is in upheaval brought on by the COVID-19 pandemic. In the U.S., millions of people have lost their jobs and nearly every activity that is not absolutely essential has been curtailed. The country is sporadically initiating a tentative re-opening, but there is considerable concern about triggering additional waves of outbreaks resulting in even more traumatic shuttering of activities. A reasonable assumption is that even when the crisis subsides or becomes at least somewhat more manageable, we will likely have to accept a future state requiring new norms. My crystal ball is no clearer than anyone else's about what this will mean to the economy and the workplace for the coming years. It's likely that there may be more virtual activities and commerce, with remote workplaces replacing some of the traditional on-site means of conducting transactions. This may require an additional set of skills beyond what is described in this book. But I believe that, as leaders grapple with new challenges left in the wake of today's upheavals, the principles I've laid out will continue to be valid and perhaps take on additional importance.

INTRODUCTION

You don't have to be a chief executive officer (CEO), a board chair, or other titled executive to be a leader. And a corollary to this statement is that there are countless people with powerful titles who are not effective leaders. I've experienced many examples of each of these types in my career, and I would bet that you have too. I invite you to join me on a journey to explore some of the key characteristics and skill sets that, in my experience, help define successful leaders and the work cultures they develop. Our focus will not be on profiling famous leaders … there are myriad biographies that have covered that information. Also, this book will not focus extensively on the foundational academic skills that an MBA program might provide, for those are already well documented and readily available. Instead, let's focus on what real-world situations leaders find themselves confronting and the critical success capabilities that sit on top of academic preparation. Whether you aspire to successfully lead a corporation, a governmental body, a church, a work team, or a volunteer group, you'll likely relate to some of the situations described along our journey together to challenges you face in your own journey.

We will be covering a lot of ground. As you work your way through the material, you may begin thinking that all of this seems much more complicated than it needs to be. Keep in mind that what I'm sharing is intended to be a tool kit, some information that may inspire new thinking, facilitate problem solving, and cause you to take a deeper dive into a subject of interest. Other leaders certainly will have different approaches. My purpose for sharing my perspectives is to stimulate you to be the best leader you can be. The world is full of problems. Many of them are self-created, stemming from bad decisions or failure to take action. Others stem from interpersonal issues brought on by poor communications or failure to develop collaborative, trusting relationships. There is much to be gained by cultivating and practicing leadership skills based on the information I've endeavored to assemble and by incorporating these skills into your own personalized leadership style and approach.

CHAPTER 1:
STARTING (OR RESTARTING) YOUR LEADERSHIP CAREER PATH

Those who aspire to become successful leaders begin or continue their journeys from a variety of perspectives.

- I am finishing my academic program soon. What opportunities should I be looking for and how do I position myself for success?

- I have been in my job for a while and I want to advance in my career. How do I prepare?

- I have experienced a career disruption. How do I find my way forward?

- I have been placed in a new leadership role and I'm finding significant challenges in knowing how to be successful.

Aspirations versus Personal Characteristics

Career success and leadership success logically begin with aligning your personal aspirations with your basic training, talents, interests, and characteristics. This is an important step that many people fail to fully consider, instead focusing narrowly on job targets based on title, salary, prestige, and perquisites. Those who have had an unplanned career disruption sometimes regret anxiously jumping into any opportunity they can find rather than stepping back to evaluate what contributed to the disruption and which opportunities may best align with their talents, aspirations, and long-term goals. This can result in suboptimal performance and failure to thrive in their roles.

While every situation has unique factors, it is important when facing either new opportunities or unanticipated adverse employment events to take the time and make the effort to analytically and emotionally understand yourself and your future aspirations. There are a variety of instruments available to assess your strongest competencies, your emotional IQ, your personality and style of leadership, your internal biases, and other factors that affect successful decision-making and the ability to influence others. In situations involving severance from employment, some companies may provide outplacement services that include assessment tools and even access to a professional coach. I urge you to ask for and avail yourself of these resources if they are available. It is also important to obtain the best understanding possible of the success factors and demands of the career or opportunity on which you wish to focus. In addition to doing your own internal research, there is great value in reaching out to build a network that includes incumbents in your position of interest, subject matter experts, and other leaders in the field you wish to pursue. You'll be surprised how many people are willing to give you their time and perspectives in helping you to shape your future.

Another significant step in your career planning and development is to understand, to the best of your ability, the operational and environmental dynamics of the industry or the specific employer of interest. For example, I spent my whole career in healthcare. Today's healthcare environment is one of rapid evolution and continuous, innovative disruption. Although the traditional hospital-based model is still a cornerstone of the industry, new healthcare delivery models such as ambulatory care centers, urgent care co-located with retail centers, and telemedicine are just a few innovative approaches that are carving out niches in competition with the traditional delivery models. Additionally, the traditional fee-for-service payment system that for decades has compensated providers based on how many services they deliver regardless of their effectiveness is slowly being displaced by an accountable-care payment system designed to place the provider at risk for patient outcomes and for management of both individual wellness and population-based chronic conditions. These paradigm shifts are stimulating a redesign of the traditional way of delivering care and this evolution is, in turn, prompting the re-creation of leadership roles with additional and different skill sets from those in the legacy system. This situation creates both opportunity and threat for those seeking to enter these new leadership roles and those who must transition from traditional leadership responsibilities into the new leadership dynamic. Those who can adapt their skills to the new-order critical success requirements will find exciting emerging opportunities. Those who fail to adapt their skills and approaches may increasingly find their leadership irrelevant.

As you ponder your current situation and evaluate opportunities for the next step in your career, consider how your personal traits and perspectives will influence your success.

Aptitude

Some questions to consider when thinking about your aptitude for a leadership role with a new employer or in a new field of work:

- Do your training and experience match the demands of the new responsibilities? Be certain you understand the accountabilities and measures of performance.

- Do the demands of the position match your interests and passion? Consider a personal inventory assessment.

- If you are succeeding someone in the position, find out whether or not that person was successful and what contributed to this outcome.

- What type and degree of support from your manager do you require? Does the opportunity match your preferred support level?

- If you have gaps in preparation and experience, is there an opportunity for further training and mentorship?

Attitude

Some questions to consider when thinking about your attitude about a leadership role with a new employer or in a new field of work:

- Are you pursuing this role because it is a passion or because of its position title and monetary rewards?

- Do you understand the personal demands required for success? Are you prepared to step up to them?

- Do you have the fortitude, perseverance, and resilience required for optimal performance?

- How do you assess this role in terms of your career progression? Is it a commitment or a steppingstone?

Adaptability

Some questions to consider when thinking about your adaptability with regard to a leadership role with a new employer or in a new field of work:

- Are you able to manage stress in a healthy, productive way?

- What is your skill level in adjusting to differing environments and environmental factors?

- Are you able to adjust to rapidly changing priorities, diverse and conflicting interests, and external demands?

Navigation Skills

Some questions to consider when thinking about your navigation skills with regard to a leadership role with a new employer or in a new field of work:

- What is your skill level in assessing and developing individualized approaches to others' personalities, leadership styles, priorities, temperaments, intrinsic biases, and relationship characteristics?

- What is your level of cultural intelligence and sensitivity?

- What is your leadership style and is it adjustable to situational and individual or group dynamics?

- What situations or personality types represent the greatest challenge or threat to your success? Can you surmount these challenges?

Personal Experience

Another career path crossroad that leaders sometimes encounter is discovering a new opportunity they find of interest or being abruptly thrust into a new opportunity. Early in my career, I encountered both of these experiences. After some years in clinical roles with relatively narrow management responsibilities, I had the opportunity to move into an administrative role at a small community hospital. I was not well prepared for the position, but excited to have the chance to advance on the career ladder. I found myself transplanted into a workplace experience dramatically different from the one I had in the clinical setting. I was asked to make decisions about issues for which I had little training or experience. I was confronted with conflicts between people and groups whose values and inherent biases I didn't fully understand and was expected to mediate successful resolutions. After a lot of learning on the job, too often through correcting course after achieving less-than-optimal results, I slowly became somewhat more competent and comfortable in the role. Some of this comfort stemmed from the fact that my boss—the CEO—was the person who actually had to answer directly to the board for management results.

So, I benefitted by having the opportunity for my occasional missteps to be corrected and to learn from them, and I had some built-in insulation from the ultimate consequences of making decisions that didn't turn out optimally. That is, until the Saturday morning I was called into the board chairman's office and informed that the board had set a change of course, that I would immediately become the interim CEO, and that I was expected to assist the board in transitioning the hospital to management by an outside company with much different management approaches and cultural identity. Suddenly, I discovered how poorly prepared I was to navigate new responsibilities without a safety net and new relationships with outside executives whose culture and expectations were dramatically different from those of my relatively brief management experience. I was caught in the middle of the demands of a number of stakeholder groups: the board, the anxious hospital staff, the community, and our patients. It was a period in which I experienced great stress and uncertainty, and I was never a big fan of either of those. As it turned out, this was only the first such wave of change in my career. It was painful in many ways, but it proved to provide a valuable touchstone. It caused me to expand my vision for my career and to leverage preparation as an antidote for anxiety. No, the anxiety didn't go away, but each subsequent period of career turbulence I experienced over the next four decades provided important lessons that better prepared me for the opportunities and challenges that followed. This was a source of empowerment. It enabled me to take steps in my career that pushed me out of my zone of comfort. It helped to build my confidence that I could succeed in more demanding roles. It also provided me with the revelation that my success was predicated on my willingness to gain new knowledge and skills.

I share these reflections with you as a preview for some of the information and exercises contained in later chapters of this book. I would also share with you that, even after a half-century of career experience, at the time I retired I was still observing similar performance challenges among emerging leaders who were not fully equipped for success. Such challenges are not confined to the healthcare field. The pace of technical and marketplace change, with the associated evolution of leadership demands, continues at an ever-accelerating rate in many fields: manufacturing, retail, education, and technology just to name a few. Couple that with the huge challenge of leading multiple generations and diverse populations of both employees and consumers with vastly differing cultural norms and expectations, and it's easy to see why career and organizational success is so difficult to achieve and sustain.

Exercise

- What real-world challenges do you now face or anticipate in your current workplace?

- What types of self-assessment have you participated in? What did the results disclose?

  - What follow-up assessment and/or skills-development steps do you plan based on the results?

- If you aspire to move up the ladder in terms of leadership position and responsibility, what are some key elements to build into your plan for success?

CHAPTER 2:
THE IMPORTANCE OF MENTORS AND NETWORKS

The predominate model of governance and management I was exposed to as I started my administrative career was patriarchal. Most administrators and CEOs were male and middle-aged or older. The management style tended to be top-down. The roles of the workforce were pretty gender-based, and there was not a lot of nuance to the way employees were managed. Looking around at other healthcare administrators of the time, I just assumed that this was the leadership style of the profession. Frankly, I didn't know what I didn't know about the science and art of management in larger organizations.

Times changed, issues changed and became more complex, and attitudes in the workforce changed during the next decade of my administrative career. As I faced new and challenging situations, I found that the old style of decision-making didn't achieve the results I was seeking. It also did not support the teamwork the organization needed in order to succeed in an increasingly challenging environment.

By the early 1980s, significant changes were made to the way Medicare paid for inpatient healthcare services delivered to their beneficiaries. Instead of allowing unlimited admissions, lengths of hospital stays, and payments, the new system set a fixed payment for each hospitalization determined by diagnostic category, regardless of length of stay. It also implemented criteria that generally had to be met in order to hospitalize a patient rather than treating the patient on an outpatient basis. These changes were accompanied by separate but similar approaches for Medicaid and commercial insurance plans. The result for hospitals was threefold: fewer admissions, lower payment, and dramatically more costly requirements for revenue-cycle management.

For hospital executives, these changes required new care-management processes and new strategies to control costs. As I was faced with the painful step of having to furlough staff due to declining revenues, the very unpopular process of educating and persuading doctors to change their patient-management approaches to accommodate the new regulatory realities and the unhappy task of explaining to our service communities why we had to implement these changes to their hospital, I came to an epiphany: I needed to learn how to better manage in difficult times.

Fortunately, my learning horizon was broadening during this time period. I was elected to some statewide boards, through which I became acquainted with colleagues who had more experience than I did in navigating the storms of leadership. At first, it was a bit humbling and awkward to ask for advice. But as my anxiety level rose, my resistance to reaching out was overcome by my need for assistance. I found it both very illuminating and very comforting to be able to talk with my colleagues about issues I was facing and to have a reliable sounding board for the actions I was considering. Honestly, it was very rare that any of these informal advisors gave me a solution I could just plug in. However, as we talked through matters, they frequently gave me the benefit of sharing similar challenges that they faced, how they proceeded, and what the results were. They often challenged me to consider more than one option and asked me if I had fully thought through all the elements of the action I was considering. Sometimes, they would just tell me that they thought I was on the right path, reassurance that made me more confident in my judgment and the resulting decisions.

Whether you are just starting out and trying to chart a course to a career, you are early in your career and considering how to move up in the ranks, you find yourself on a course change, or you are in a leadership role and faced with challenges, developing a network of mentors and colleagues who can provide guidance and input has many benefits.

- For those seeking a job, well-connected and well-regarded colleagues can open doors and also provide important reference support that adds substance to your candidacy. There really is strength in numbers, as this group can greatly broaden your search efforts through connections that they have.

- For those experiencing an unplanned course change, whether through lay-off or through severance, seeking the counsel of others who have either experienced this or have guided others through the process of finding the next job can be very stabilizing. For most people, this experience is traumatic and anxiety producing. It is a time when emotion can overcome intellect. Having an experienced colleague help you design the search process and identify other support resources, as well as coach you to make sure the process stays on track, can greatly increase the chance of successfully moving on.

- For those who—like I have—find themselves in a leadership role facing major challenges, your colleagues can help you avoid tunnel vision and can be very useful in helping you think through alternatives.

A caveat: Select your mentors and network of colleagues carefully. Avoid those who have a tendency to try to solve problems for you and those who may have a bias that may limit your thinking. Seek out those with open minds, credible experience, and strong analytic and people skills.

Another caveat: In weighing possible actions, don't substitute seeking outside advice for the need to carefully solicit and listen to the counsel of your internal stakeholders and subject matter experts. The best guidance doesn't always come from outside consultants or people with impressive titles.

Exercise

Consider the areas of the current state of your career.

- Where do you find yourself needing guidance?

- What knowledge or experiential deficits come into play?

- What is the breadth of your network of colleagues whom you can call upon for counsel or assistance?

- How will you sustain and grow existing relationships?

Now consider ways you can increase your network.

- Are there contacts within your alma mater?

- Are there professional organizations you can join through which a new base of colleagues can be developed?

- Are there volunteer or service opportunities related to your field of interest, through which you can develop new professional relationships?

- Are there people who might have recently retired from the field who might become mentors?

CHAPTER 3:
LEADERSHIP CULTURE

One of the lessons I learned—and relearned multiple times—is that while an individual leader's skills are very important, it is the organizational culture that most often drives success or failure. This is as true for leaders in lower-level management roles as it is for the highest positions of leadership. Organizational cultures can and will take on many undesirable characteristics if they are not developed and nurtured. They may become complacent, self-serving, and even toxic. At the organization level, this can be reflected in significant dysfunction: difficulty in hiring and retaining well-prepared staff, internal conflict, adverse workforce actions, errors, legal actions, low consumer trust and ratings, and, ultimately, poor overall performance. When this happens at the unit or departmental level of the organization, it's often reflected in conflicts with other departments, finger pointing, undermining, and low productivity. When it happens at the highest levels of management, it can become very public and may be career limiting for top leaders. The accountability eventually lands there at some point. On the other hand, an organization that has successfully infused its culture with leadership skills and empowerment often demonstrates high levels of employee satisfaction and engagement, superior productivity and quality, low turnover, strong pride in its work, and a loyal consumer base.

If you are a new leader or new to your current leadership role, how can you build a highly functional, highly engaged team? Let's start by exploring some defining characteristics of a culture of leadership. This exploration may begin with a review of your own experiences with workplace leaders. What leadership characteristics inspired you as a team member? Conversely, what characteristics led to a negative experience? What kind of employee culture and work environment resulted from these leadership experiences and how did those affect the success of the organization you worked for? How did those experiences either motivate you to higher job satisfaction and performance or, conversely, discourage you?

Good leadership is not monolithic. It can be exhibited amid a variety of individual leader personality types, leadership styles, and academic and experiential preparations. It can also be demonstrated at any organizational level or with any job title. To understand how leaders are viewed as successful, I find it helpful to first consider the attributes of a highly functioning workplace culture. This culture is one that is most likely to be composed of people who say they enjoy working for their organization. They feel appreciated, take pride in their efforts, and are committed to achieving a high level of quality. The organization they work for is most likely one that achieves a high degree of customer satisfaction and loyalty.

I think it is safe to say that most of us would like to work in this type of setting. Many of us have worked in organizations led by good people with good intentions, but we might not give that workplace culture very high ratings. In an age of intense competition to recruit and retain competent and dedicated staff, failure to achieve a workplace setting in which employees are both engaged and loyal is a major impediment to success.

So how do the high-performing enterprises achieve and sustain strong employee and customer engagement? There can be many effective approaches; however, in organizations with larger employee populations and more ethnic, generational, experiential, and training diversity, this must be an intentional and sustained process. It starts at the top of the organization, but it must cascade uniformly throughout the leadership of the organization—a culture of leadership!

What are some of the characteristics of a successful leadership culture? What would employees and employee teams say about it? This list is not exhaustive, and I invite you to add to it.

- There is a sense of mutual trust and respect between organizational layers and among employee teams.

- Staff members feel respected and appreciated for their knowledge, talent, and achievement.

- Employees in all capacities understand their roles and responsibilities, and how their performance is measured.

- Performance is consistently, fairly, and objectively measured. Rewards are results-oriented and designed to promote effective collaboration among teams, in addition to superior individual performance.

- Employees are aware of and feel supported by the organization's policies and procedures, and sense that these are administered justly and consistently applied.

- They are reliably informed of how their organization is performing and how they and their teams are contributing.

- They feel that their proximal leaders, as well as top management, are trustworthy, provide support for their success, and demonstrate interest in their career development.

- They feel that their work environment is safe and that they are protected from dysfunctional behaviors such as bullying and harassment.

- When they encounter problems or differences of opinions, they know how to effectively work through them and feel supported as they do.

- They feel well informed by, and have a sense of connection with, their own and other managers.

- They feel committed to best practices and continual improvement of the work they do.

We will circle back to some of the practical aspects of the process of developing and sustaining a leadership culture in later chapters. In chapter four, let's continue our journey by looking at some of the challenges of leading and how to build skills in navigating them successfully.

Exercise

- Describe a leader who most inspired you. What was that person's personality and style? Why did this person positively influence you?

- Describe a leader who caused you to feel disengaged and unmotivated. Give examples of that person's leadership that represented a disconnection with your aspirations.

- What attributes of a successful leadership culture would you add to the list above?

CHAPTER 4:
EFFECTIVE LEADERSHIP—
REAL-WORLD CHALLENGES

There can be no question about the importance of the education provided by formal degree programs that prepare leaders to understand the structure and principles that underpin successful organizational management. Such programs prepare leaders to have a strong grasp of finance, the principles of human resource management, legal and regulatory requirements, risk management, revenue-cycle management, and a myriad of other skills that are intrinsic to managing a successful business enterprise. The ability to analyze income statements and balance sheets, quality and risk analyses, employee-engagement reports, incident reports, and the other tools of tracking the status of the enterprise are crucial to the success of leaders. They represent a basic foundation for much of the day-to-day and month-to-month management accountabilities within organizations.

A comment I have heard many times as I have mentored leaders is, "Okay, I feel that I have good competency in the areas of focus in my formal training, but I've run into situations at work for which I don't feel well prepared." To paraphrase, it's usually something like, "I feel like I've been thrown into the deep end of the pool!" Here are some examples of situations that, if not handled well, can become career trap doors:

- Navigating internally competing strategic and operational tribal interests of employee groups

- Successfully managing relationships with senior staff such as your bosses and the board

- Effectively making and communicating decisions

- Taking timely and effective action on mission-critical or ethical issues

- Developing engaged and effective teams and achieving required performance in a rapidly changing environment

- Creating and sustaining a culture of improvement aligned with key organizational strategies and tactics

Certainly, there are others. I invite you to reflect on your own experiences and add to the list. It is difficult to teach people how to deal with these types of challenges. There are different personality types, management styles, personal experiences, values, and biases that assure that there is no one specific way to manage them. But it is possible to help developing leaders arrive at internal thought processes and approaches that they can use as they build experience in working through challenging situations. In the following chapters, we will explore some approaches and techniques that I have found helpful in my career … and I often arrived at them the hard way.

Exercise

- Describe one or more trap-door situations that you have witnessed, experienced, or that you worry about your ability to manage; situations that kept you awake at night or that you dreaded to have to face; situations that made you worry about your own viability in the organization.

- What other types of leadership challenges occur to you to add to the list above?

CHAPTER 5:
AN ORGANIZATIONAL CULTURE OF ENGAGEMENT AND IMPROVEMENT

Let's start by addressing the last trap-door item listed in chapter four—creating and sustaining a culture of improvement—because developing and nurturing such a culture is fundamental to effectively addressing the others. The attributes described in chapter three constitute some of the building blocks of a workforce culture that is focused not only on performing at its best level today, but also on how to continually improve. Top performers take pride in the results of their efforts and also in working together to keep themselves and their organization at the top of their field. Whatever rung on the leadership ladder you may occupy, building and nurturing this culture will enhance the satisfaction of your work group, avoid many problems inherent in teams, make the problems you do encounter more manageable, and distinguish you and your group as trustworthy, high-quality performers.

When describing individual employees, teams of employees, or a full workforce of employees, the term engagement may generally be used to characterize their passion for and level of satisfaction in the work they perform, their commitment to those they serve and to their employer, their sense of ownership of their tasks and their results, their resilience when challenges occur, and their level of trust in and commitment to those who manage them and to their co-workers. These are employees who will drive high levels of organizational performance and customer loyalty. They will provide the foundation for an enjoyable workplace experience. And they will help sustain a culture that doesn't abide low quality work or toxic behavior.

So, as a leader, whether your office is in the C-Suite or you are a front-line manager, how do you create, nurture, and sustain this type of work force? As you might expect, it's a journey of doing many things well and sustaining that level of performance over time. At the risk of oversimplifying, I offer a few basic components.

Set a Clear Vision for the Workforce Operation and Culture

Just as architects design a structure before it is constructed, it is important for those who are tasked with building a competent and cohesive workforce to have a well-developed blueprint to guide them. So, if you are a CEO or company president, it is incumbent on you to develop and articulate the vision for how members of the organization's workforce experience their roles and their relationships with their co-workers. Moreover, it is critical that in developing this vision, you consider the experience that consumers of your services and products will have as they interact with your organization. How will they rate the level of professionalism, quality, courtesy, compassion, and teamwork that they observe? The vision you create should incorporate clear expectations and measures for these service attributes.

In most instances, as you assume your management role you won't just inherit an optimal operating environment. You'll likely have to build and sustain it. This effort is not a one-time initiative. It is not a program you buy from a consultant or dust off and trot out once per year. It should be an ongoing part of the organization's strategic and operational plans. Viewed from the top level of the enterprise, it should provide a common understanding across the organization of day-to-day behavioral expectations that guide and motivate it to high work performance and satisfaction. Viewed from a middle-management or line-management perspective, it should be a platform from which the manager models and reinforces the vision and holds teams accountable to its standards. From a workforce perspective, it should provide the rules of the road for how all levels of employees interact with each other and with those they serve. When developed and managed optimally, every staff member should honestly be able to say, "I am appreciated and respected by my coworkers and by my employer."

Hire for Success

Finding and retaining competent employees is a daunting task these days. In many industries, there are large numbers of job offerings for which there are often too-few qualified applicants. But a saying that I strongly believe is, "The only thing worse than having no one to fill a role is having the wrong person filling the role." The most fundamental element of creating and sustaining a high-quality and engaged workforce is hiring the right people. Some leaders are fortunate enough to work in organizations that have highly capable and sophisticated human resource management support to assist in the selection process. For those leaders who are more on their own in selecting new team members, here are some elements I would suggest you consider building into your selection process.

Screen applicants carefully to vet their training, experience, and previous employment history. This should include any red flags like unexplained gaps in employment, short-duration engagements, or professional disciplinary events.

Be certain that each position has a well-developed job description. The tasks and roles expected, the standards of performance with appropriate metrics, the work-production relationships to other employee groups, and the behavioral standards should be clear.

Include on the selection committee appropriate members of the team(s) with which the selected leader will work closely. Assure that those participating in the interview have been well versed in the types of questions that are legally permissible and that they are prepared to ask questions that are complementary to the overall goals of the interview.

Use behavioral-based interview techniques. These involve open-ended questions and discussions that encompass operational issues that are relevant to the organization's real-life workplace. They are designed to help interviewers understand the interviewee's base of experience, emotional IQ, personality, maturity, leadership style, team compatibility, and resilience. They are often targeted to specific challenges that the organization is subject to or is currently experiencing. They also may focus on specific attributes that the organization's management is trying to build into the company culture. For example, the questioner may ask the interviewee to describe a situation in which there was a conflict in priorities between their area of responsibility and someone else's. How did the candidate manage the conflict and was it resolved successfully? What did the candidate learn? Assessing these traits, in addition to the other skills the position requires, can assist those making the selection to assure that the person selected will have the best chance for success. This assessment process can also help build the accountable workplace culture the organization is seeking, by holding selection team members responsible for choosing the best collaborative partner and then to support that person's success.

Hire for retention. It is important to understand the mindset and goals of the applicant. The cost of training a new employee is often staggering. The more complex the role—and leadership roles are usually complex—the more costly the orientation and training is. So turnover is very expensive for those positions. Unlike a bygone era in which leaders often worked for one or only a few employers in their careers, today's leadership talent may assume they will work for many employers. Finding the right person for a leadership role, one who is seeking professional and personal goals aligned with the goals of the organization, will increase the chance for a long-term, successful employment relationship. And the effort doesn't conclude at that point. It is critically important that the employer provides ongoing support to assure that the orientation and enculturation processes for the new leader are successful.

Build a Process to Develop and Sustain the Envisioned Culture

Each organization and its leadership will decide what specific elements make the most sense in developing and sustaining its leadership culture, because there must be a balance between investment of time and resources and the return realized from that investment. Larger organizations with multiple divisions or departments will probably benefit from having a more-robust approach than smaller organizations with fewer units and a more homogenous workgroup. For descriptive purposes, I will provide a more expansive set of suggestions based on a larger, more complex employee base. Smaller organizations may wish to tailor these suggestions to fit their resource capabilities and needs.

If the organization has not completed an employee-engagement assessment within the past year, this would be a good initial step. The assessment tool selected should demonstrate proven results, as attested to by other users. The deliverables should include assistance with interpretation of results and recommendations for follow-up. The instruments should provide the ability to report assessment responses sorted by proximal leader, as well as at the organization level. The questions should be well developed for clarity of interpretation, both for the leaders and for those responding to the questions. The assessment tool and those who administer and help interpret it must have credibility with those taking the assessment. Employees should feel assured that their responses are confidential and anonymous. Top leaders must assure the integrity of these protections. They must clearly and convincingly communicate that the assessment process and the associated performance-improvement processes are anonymous and are directed at enhancing employee satisfaction and at achieving an optimal workplace culture.

Once results are obtained (and compared to previous engagement survey results, if applicable), top leadership should spend the required time and effort to assure its thorough and accurate understanding of the data. Depending on the assessment tool used, the results should provide important insights into:

- what employees find to be the most important drivers of satisfaction and how well the organization is meeting their expectations

- the leadership strengths and weaknesses of individual leaders as viewed by the staff who report to them

- the staff's perspective on key hot-button issues such as organizational integrity and workplace safety

- the cohesiveness of their proximal team

- the quality of interactional relationship of their team with other teams in the organization

Senior leaders should then develop a plan for the performance-improvement (PI) process and how the results are to be shared. The PI process, as well as associated communications, should be consistent throughout the organization. It should include uniform and specific leadership accountabilities and metrics that are built into the organization's performance reviews for managers.

A key element of the PI process is assurance that those in leadership roles have the education and training necessary to be successful in understanding the results, in understanding their roles and responsibilities as improvement managers, and in communicating in a manner that is consistent across the organization. Leaders should be provided with necessary ongoing support from those to whom they report. It should be understood throughout the organization that the results of the assessment are designed to drive improvement by giving leaders a better understanding of what their teams feel is most important to them and how well their team and the organization is performing on those measures. It is also important that all staff understand the big-picture processes involved in the improvement plan and see the plan actually being carried out as it was described to them.

The PI process will be individualized to the organization's needs and existing culture. Some of the elements of the plan will include the following.

The Performance Improvement Process

Identify the key drivers of employee engagement. While the responses to all questions are important, the volume of information to absorb may be overwhelming and even counterproductive. It is likely that there will be some variations of response among different employee groups. It can be easy to get lost in a forest of information produced by an assessment, causing leaders to become mired in minutia. With assistance from skilled human resource and testing professionals, it should be possible to determine a few key questions and responses that represent the most impactful perspectives of employees and groups. Effective action taken to address these key matters will most fundamentally drive improvement in employee engagement.

It may be necessary to conduct some employee and leadership focus groups to assure that those who are tasked with designing the PI approach have the best possible understanding of what messages the responses are providing.

Once the key drivers are clarified, look for common issues, themes, and sources of variance from best practice. Is there a need for certain types of individual or group leadership education? If yours is a multiple-shift organization, are the responses more pronounced on one shift than others? Are there certain employee groups whose responses are more declarative than others? Do the employees of certain managers show variation in their responses compared to those of other managers? Identifying commonalities, as well as variances, will help target the PI efforts more productively.

While implementing the analysis and planning the PI process, regular and consistent communication with employees is important in order to maintain their trust in the integrity of the process and the work product it produces. In organizations with multiple management levels, mid-level managers should have appropriate information about the results and the improvement process before widespread sharing occurs throughout the organization. This gives the managers an opportunity to process the information and to understand their roles and accountabilities in the communication and PI processes, assuring that they are not blindsided.

The PI process, which can be tailored to fit the organization, may include some or all of the following steps:

- Survey results analysis and plan preparation by the senior management team. The plan preparation may either be robust at this level or more instructional, leaving the development of plan detail as a responsibility of the mid-management team, in order to foster their ownership of the plan and the results. Whichever approach is taken, senior leadership must own it and support it.

- Communicating survey results, the planning process, and timelines with the general employee population. This is a crucial step, because employees will watch to see how closely what they observe in the process matches the description they were provided. A critical success factor for the effort is maintaining trust in the process and those who are leading it. It is at this point that the senior leader should make it clear that employee-engagement initiatives—both the survey process and the improvement efforts—will be ongoing into the future rather than a one-time activity. It should also be emphasized that the efforts will be organization-wide, with everyone having a role in driving the success of the efforts.

- Executing the plan. The remainder of the PI activities—and remember that they are perpetual—involves diligently executing the plan, periodically reassessing progress-to-plan using multiple feedback approaches, and communicating the progress with all teams. This includes problem solving and refining the process if concerns arise. As mentioned earlier, employees want to feel that they are valued and respected. The engagement survey should give management a sense of the degree to which that is being accomplished. Thus, a derivative of the employee-engagement process is developing a set of workplace norms—those policies, procedures, and behavioral standards that constitute the rules of the road for how the people of the workplace interact with each other. Some of the most important expectations most of us have of our workplace setting include:

  - I want to know how my performance is evaluated

  - I want to feel appreciated for my talents and efforts

  - I want to feel respected by others I work with

  - I want to be able to count on the ethics and integrity of everyone in the organization

  - I want to be able to count on my co-workers to produce a high standard of work performance

I'm sure there are others that you feel are important to you. Anyone who has had much experience in a workplace setting probably has stories to tell of organizational variances from these ideals. Without rigorous development and consistent reinforcement of behavioral standards, the workplace norm may deteriorate into a default state driven by the daily rush of activities. This often leads to conflicts, lack of teamwork, disrespect for each other, and a disengaged desire to just get through the day. I don't think most people intentionally adopt these behaviors. Instead, the behaviors derive from long-standing ways of interaction among people with different personalities, values, tribal customs (we'll get more into that topic later), hierarchies, generational perspectives, sensitivities, past disputes, and a variety of other individual differences.

For discussion purposes, let's assume that the desired expectations listed above are the key drivers for employee engagement in your organization and the current state is that, while there are some teams who feel that their expectations are being met satisfactorily, there are others who might not agree. They may feel they have been treated disrespectfully or even that they have been bullied. They may feel that those who cut corners are not held accountable. They may feel that superior effort and good results are not recognized. Developing an environment that supports consistent behavioral standards throughout the organization requires that several elements are put into place. These elements include the following.

- Policies and procedures must document and support the behavioral expectations. These expectations should be standardized from the highest level of the organization (governance and administration), through all management levels and throughout the rank and file. It is not enough that these policies are published and only looked at when an adverse event occurs. All members of the organization should have regular education and reminders about them. And they must be consistently applied.

- Through multiple venues, top management of the organization should find ways to reiterate, reinforce, reward, and, of course, exhibit the cultural attributes being developed. The attributes should be integrated into the employee-performance reviews.

- It may be helpful to develop behavioral covenants, which are statements to which everyone in the organization pledges. For example, using some of the expectations above:

  - I treat all co-workers with respect, as I wish to be treated.

  - I follow the highest standards of ethics and integrity as I do my work.

  - I accept personal accountability for my behaviors, interactions with others, and the results of my work.

  - I always strive to be honest and respectful in my communications.

  - I am committed to providing the highest quality in the services I deliver and to consistently strive toward personal and organizational performance improvement.

Such covenants can be commemorated in various forms and at various sites in the workplace, such as bulletin boards, newsletters, locker rooms, and so on. They can be printed on the backs of employee-identification badges. They should be reviewed and refined, as needed, and signed off on annually by each employee during the performance-management process. They also prove useful when there has been a variance—perceived or real—in someone's behavior. They provide a clear basis for discussion about the variance and a road map for resolution.

Based on experience in some of the hospitals for which I had oversight responsibility, I have high praise for the work that Vanderbilt University Medical Center has done in helping organizations develop a culture of respect. The training received from this organization, which spanned from board members to administration to hospital leadership and through the ranks, was transformative. The resultant empowered culture was very much reflected in the staff's interactions with each other and with the patients they served. It was also validated by the high scores achieved in employee-engagement assessments conducted over multiple years.

Train Staff at All Levels to Have Crucial Conversations

Training staff at all levels in the art of having crucial conversations is fundamental to the success of sustaining a workplace environment of quality and respect. Things don't always go perfectly. People don't always communicate constructively or even appropriately. Being human, we all have our off days and wish for a do-over with people to whom we relate. Policies establish behavioral expectations. Covenants specify the workplace values and norms that employees can expect as they interact with each other. But if a staff member perceives unfair or disrespectful treatment from another staff member, how this situation is communicated and resolved determines what the state of the workplace culture really is. For less-assertive staff members, having the template and training for how to properly discuss inter-relational problems provides empowerment and a sanctioned way to address grievances. For the person who may be the subject of the grievance, the expression of the aggrieved person is the recognized response that is sanctioned by the organization. It isn't a gotcha. It creates a safe platform for discussion that optimizes the chance for one-to-one resolution, rather than escalation or allowing the problem to slide into toxicity. The resulting discussion is standardized and conducted with established ground rules. This is particularly important when the person who is perceived as being unfair or disrespectful holds a position of authority over the person who is aggrieved.

Organizations will benefit in many ways from training all staff members in the art of having crucial conversations. Such training may reduce the likelihood of lawsuits, employee group actions, proliferation of unseemly behaviors, toxic workplace consequences, and staff turnover. As importantly, it may reduce the chance of poor organizational performance and costly errors. The book, *Crucial Conversations: Tools for Talking When Stakes are High,* by Kerry Patterson, Joseph Grenny, Ron McMillan, and Al Switzler, outlines the principles of conducting crucial conversations: how to set them up, conduct them, and get to desired results. By creating a norm that empowers every employee to say to a peer or to someone in a position of authority, "I felt you did not respect me when you scolded me in front of my team. Could we sit down together and discuss this issue and how we might manage future issues together more respectfully?" As the training gives each person the skills needed to have such conversations, the organizational culture not only becomes one of stronger engagement, but also one of higher quality.

Human nature being what it is, sometimes crucial conversations don't resolve a problem. At that point it is critical that the person or persons at the next level follow policies, procedures, and protocols of the organization consistently and objectively to bring issues to resolution. Yes, this escalation may require its own use of crucial conversations. All who participate in or observe the matter should recognize this process to be one of credibility and integrity. The results should advance organizational improvement and should serve to reinforce organizational values.

An important element in assuring a workplace in which staff members feel they are respected is how the organization deals with adverse events such as errors and resultant harm. The cause of such events might run the spectrum from human error all the way to criminal actions. The consequences of such events might range from none to minor to significant to catastrophic. Their source may be carelessness, negligence, or intentional misbehavior. However, systemic failures in the production processes may also be a source, creating a built-in risk of error. If the organization handles adverse events in subjective, arbitrary fashion with consequences that vary from person to person, the result may be that staff members hide mistakes, become risk averse to the point of reduced functionality, and disengage from ownership of their results.

Note:

Those of us who have spent time in healthcare management recognize the term Just Culture. It was first used in a 2001 report by David Marx, who is the CEO of Outcome Engenuity, LLC, and is associated with the Center for Patient Safety. This report became integrated into the base of practice around the patient safety-improvement movement. It spurred a refinement to the approach of analyzing and setting consequences for adverse events. I won't attempt to detail the contents of the report, but would instead encourage you to conduct your own review of it and the subsequent literature that represents the basis of the Just Culture movement. I would note that, fortuitously, this refinement in approach intersects well with efforts to build an engaged and quality-focused workforce. Through its application and refinements, managers have come to recognize that there are categories of error that require different actions. Filtering this through my own experiences, I would observe that there are honest errors, for example those that are systemic in nature: rush and overload situations, incomplete or ineffective training, staffing shortages, equipment malfunctions, poor labeling, and so on. There are also negligence-related adverse events: the person making the error wasn't paying appropriate attention or was sloppy in doing a task for which he or she was properly trained. Finally, there are willful acts and reckless behaviors: acts that reasonable people would conclude were the fault of the person committing them. With appropriate analysis and parsing of circumstances of the adverse event, the consequences to the involved staff member can be tailored. If a systemic issue has caused or significantly contributed to the event, it may be necessary to initiate a performance-improvement process on the dysfunctional system, retrain of the staff member, or perform other actions that address the system flaw. If the staff member was negligent, a degree of discipline may be required that fits the seriousness of the negligence and its outcome. If the staff member was willfully negligent or reckless, the most serious consequence is warranted. By making the effort to analyze each adverse event using processes that staff recognize as objective and focused on improvement, while holding everyone accountable for best practice, the organization accomplishes not only a reduction in avoidable errors, but also nurturing of an engaged employee culture in which staff learns and improves from mistakes rather than hiding them.

Maintain Multiple Lines of Internal Communication

Stay in touch. Communicate, communicate, and communicate again! One of the perceived shortcomings of management that employees and teams most frequently cite is lack of communication. If you are the object of that concern, that can be frustrating, because you may believe that you have been very open and accessible to staff. But while doing an occasional town hall meeting and sending out a newsletter is fine (and necessary), top leaders must maintain multiple channels of communication with staff in order to achieve an open and trusting relationship. And remember, many organizations have four or five generations of staff members. What works well for one generation may fall flat for another.

In my experience, one very effective method of communicating is walking the hallways. If the organization has multiple shifts, that means regularly showing up at each. Different leaders have different styles of communication with teams. As a CEO and member of executive teams, I regularly rounded on all units of the hospitals and on all shifts. I often had with me information to be shared about our operations, new policies, new issues affecting us, and other topics to keep them apprised of important issues. At other times, I simply stopped by their locations and had conversations about how their work was going, what challenges they were facing, what ideas they had, what they had questions about or needed more information about, what the gossip mill was churning out, or simply how their son or daughter was doing in college. I also tried to convey to the teams that I understood and respected their departmental policies and practices. For example, in preparation for engaging staff members on the adult psychiatric inpatient unit, I took Mandt training (instruction on situation de-escalation and management techniques) with their group so that I would not be a danger to them if a patient situation got out of hand while I was on the unit. I had lunch (or dinner or midnight snacks) with employee groups. I rounded at many of the medical-specialist offices and developed an understanding of what their issues and challenges were.

These relational efforts are not confined to top management. If you are a line leader or department manager, chances are that you are also a subject matter expert for the team(s) you manage. It's just as vital for you to have meaningful dialogue and a strong relationship with members of your work group. The further up the management ladder your position is, the more you may find that your grasp of the operational and relationship challenges of work teams is superficial and sometimes totally lacking. If you are not diligent about becoming and remaining educated about the real environment in which these teams operate, you may discover that your credibility as a leader diminishes. So, however you choose to do it, you need incorporate the most effective approaches to remaining in touch with your workforce. And remember, the interactions you have with them should be two-way. You are there to answer questions, to listen, and to learn, and to give them feedback, perhaps more than to impart information. Finally, harking back to the respectful culture you seek to develop and sustain, the more frequent and substantive interaction you have with members of your workforce, the more likely it is that you will know what concerns are out there before the regular employee-engagement assessments are done. And the more likely it is that your employees will trust you enough to respond honestly and to believe that you will too.

Exercise

Look at the examples of behavioral covenants listed earlier in the chapter. From the standpoint of an employee of an organization, what are your top expectations for yourself and for others you inter-act with in the workplace? Discuss how organization-wide account-ability for these behavioral expectations provides a platform for quality performance and quality improvement.

CHAPTER 6:
NAVIGATING A NEW LEADERSHIP ENVIRONMENT

New leaders, as well as those newly transplanted from other environments, often encounter challenges for which their training and experience haven't adequately prepared them. To paraphrase frequent concerns expressed by these newly minted executives:

- The environment, the personalities, and the dynamics are alien to me.

- I don't know how to prioritize everything that is coming at me.

- The priorities I've been given keep changing.

- I'm caught in the middle between team members who are in conflict with one another.

- It isn't clear how success is measured in my role.

- Communication among those to whom I am accountable is dysfunctional.

- My boss is not helpful or supportive. I'm left to twist in the wind.

A variety of factors may contribute to this common malady. First, the new environment is often the domain of tenured leaders whose success has been honed and solidified through individual approaches that work for them. Thus, attempts to change their views or behaviors will rarely result in resolution. Second, these leaders are prone to have some of the same strategic and tribal perspectives as those that will be discussed in chapter 7. Those perspectives, too, are generally hard-wired. Third, the higher up the organizational ladder leaders reside, the more resolute they may be in their ways of decision-making and relating to others. Finally, top management's ability to achieve optimal synchrony of strong personalities and diverse organizational challenges is finite. Thus, while it is very important for senior management to mentor and support the success of organizational leaders who are new to their roles, new leaders must sometimes seek out additional knowledge and skills as part of their maturation process. They must also learn new strategies to accomplish their responsibilities in the face of less-than-perfect interpersonal situations.

In her book, *Managing Up: How to Move Up, Win at Work, and Succeed with Any Type of Boss*, Mary Abbajay provides a compendium of situations that staff members—including leaders—may need to learn to navigate when dealing with those to whom they are accountable. In it, she provides her perspective on the following topics.

- Types of Bosses. Anyone with workplace experience will recognize the spectrum of styles and behaviors examined. Is your boss introverted or extroverted? A doer or a delegator? A pragmatist or a disciplinarian? Understanding the personality and style of your boss and the associated strategies of relating to that type of person is essential to a successful relationship and to accomplishing goals. Ms. Abbajay provides some excellent examples of types of bosses and associated strategies to align operational and relational efforts with them.

- What is Important to Your Boss … What Drives Behavior? It's a great question that many people fail to consider as they ponder how to forge an effective relationship with the person who judges their performance. It's easy, especially in times of emotional duress, to get caught up in superficial approaches to make your boss like you more. But at a functional level, remembering that most bosses have a person or persons to whom they are accountable (higher-level managers, boards, shareholders, and stakeholders), it is very important to consider what your boss's priorities are and the outcomes your boss is looking for. These priorities may be based on their own performance reviews and rewards, organizational gain or risk, self-fulfillment, or other drivers.

- Tactics for:

  - Successful working partnerships

  - Mitigating difficulties in a challenging relationship

  - Surviving and thriving

As I read this book, I repeatedly identified its relevance to interactions I have experienced and that I have witnessed my colleagues trying to work through. Not just with our bosses, but also with other leaders with whom we must work to accomplish our accountabilities. By understanding the characteristics and perspectives of other leaders, we can be better prepared to strategize how to come to agreement on decisions.

Exercise

I encourage you to read Ms. Abbajay's book. Consider your own personality traits, values, and approaches to work. Then consider those of bosses or other people with whom you have regular transactions.

- What personality types and workplace approaches have you found to be the most challenging in others?

- What thoughts do you have about how best to mitigate these challenges in order to accomplish required tasks and also to relieve your stress in dealing with them?

CHAPTER 7:
NAVIGATING INTERNALLY COMPETING STRATEGIC AND TRIBAL INTERESTS

If you work in an organization that has multiple levels of management, a number of departments containing people with various types of specialized expertise, and work products that depend on people at all levels and of all disciplines to interact effectively, it's likely that you will run into competing strategic priorities and what I categorize as tribal interests.

Strategic Interests

Organizations have budgets that are finite, which means that not all of the interests of each and every department or team is likely to be prioritized and funded to the degree that everyone would wish. Team A might wish to have a new piece of capital equipment. Team B might wish to invest in an expensive marketing campaign. Team C might wish to add staff. Each team strongly values its own priorities. By extension, each team will make its best pitch to top management that the investment it wants will bring the greatest strategic value to the organization.

There are other ways in which strategic-interest competition plays out. Groups may compete for power in the organization. Or they may compete over who does what or who has to do what. They may compete over workplace policies. Regardless of the source of competition or conflict, groups usually feel a high degree of passion for their particular cause or point of view.

Tribal Interests

Groups or individuals who share certain commonalities such as training, professional status, generational identity, core values, tenure with the organization, or other traits or experiences in common with each other sometimes exhibit tribal characteristics and interests. They often hold strong views of what is most important in the workplace, who is the authority over a matter, and how work gets done. These strong views sometimes come into conflict with the strongly held views of other tribes. Harking back on my career experience, here are some examples from the world of healthcare:

- Best care versus Cost of Care. In my view, these two positions are not mutually exclusive, but discussions between persons whose primary accountability is financially focused and those who are accountable for delivering care to patients can quickly go off the rails.

- Growth versus Compliance Roles. Those who are responsible in their roles to help their organization increase business and grow resources may sometimes run into some difficult realities when they enter into discussions with compliance staff, whose role is to assure that the organization doesn't violate laws and regulations. And many times, because law and regulations are sometimes interpretive, the decision boils down to a judgment call rather than a clear binary decision.

- Professional Identity. Professional tribes within healthcare include governing body, administration, clinical professions (physician, nurse, other clinical and technical staff), executive staff, non-clinical teams, daytime teams, nighttime teams, and many others. Their roles entail expertise, historical traditions, perspectives, values, biases, and rituals that can create conflict when interacting with other groups with different professional identities and inherent traits.

- Generational identity. Larger organizations may have members of four or even five generations in the workforce. In general, each generation has its own commonalities, values, preferred ways of learning, preferred ways of working, preferred ways of communicating, and sense of which management approaches motivate and which approaches chafe. They may differ in opinion about what is personally satisfying or irritating about their work, and about the types of rewards they find most meaningful. Trying to lead and engage all the groups using a monolithic approach will often result in suboptimal results and frustration.

If you find yourself interacting with someone from another group with points of view that differ from your own, it is often very helpful to step back and think through the perspectives that shape their position. With what work group does that person most closely identify and what is that group's traditional values and biases? To whom is that person directly accountable? By what measure is that person's performance evaluated? What level of expertise does the person have in the contended issue? What experience is that person able to draw on to demonstrate support for the position? Is the person's style of interaction to aggressively assert a position and only compromise when provided with credible evidence of a different position, or is the person more open-minded? Based on the person's professional identity, what type of supporting evidence for your position is likely to be credible? If there is a generational perspective barrier, how can you frame the discussion in a manner that resonates? The list of scenarios is boundless. The point is that the better you can understand what shapes the perspectives that the person brings to the table, the better you can do the work before negotiating that enables you to frame a position that is more likely to lead to consensus.

Exercise

You are the recently appointed director of business operations of a small university. You were promoted to this position by a provost who joined the university six months ago. Your promotion was part of a reorganization of administrative functions to enable new strategic advances. You had most recently been in a lower-level student body-management position with the university for eight years after receiving your graduate degree from the university. You are elated by your recent advancement and hope that it is a step toward future promotions, but somewhat awed by the challenges the new provost has given you to take the lead in advancing her vision for the university's growth. The provost has laid out a directive to increase the proportion of virtual instruction in order to better compete with other academic centers and to reduce the university's overhead costs associated with in-class instruction. This shift in strategy will require investments in new technology, training of the professors in use of the technology and new techniques of instruction, assuring that the changes will not have an adverse impact on accreditation, and designing and rolling out a new marketing effort. There will be a financial impact due to the expense of these investments coupled with a reduction in room and board and ancillary revenues associated with in-house instruction. Your colleagues who make up the transitional task force are a long-tenured director of graduate studies, a director of finance who has fifteen years of experience in the role, a director of marketing who just joined the university, and the appointed liaison representing the university professors.

Assume the following profiles:

- The provost has relevant experience in a small-college setting. She also has a background as a small-college professor of business studies. She is accountable to a board of regents that has charged her with successfully growing the university's footprint and student base.

- The director of graduate studies is the oldest member of your group of colleagues. Due to his tenure, he is usually assertive about his beliefs and is often given deference by those who must interact with him. He is not a fan of technology and built his career on face-to-face instruction and management. He views his responsibility as protecting the reputation and integrity of the graduate programs.

- The director of finance is a no-nonsense middle-aged man who came to the university from a similar role in the business world. He has very strong financial-management skills, however he is viewed by both those who work for him and those who must transact with him as not very flexible. He sees his role as guarding the college treasury.

- The director of marketing is a high-energy, very creative young woman. After graduating from college, she has had two fairly short job stints in high-budget retail marketing positions, where her creativity and energy helped her become successful.

- The academic liaison was appointed by the new provost, with recommendations from the professorial group. He has been a professor of social sciences at the university for twenty years, starting immediately after finishing his graduate degree. He is sociable, but he carries an aura of old-school mannerisms. He strongly values respect for the profession and sees his role as a protector of the dignity and values of the academic group, as well as the integrity of the university's instructional reputation.

Consider the following questions.

- How would you, as the leader and facilitator of the transition, prepare for your meetings with the task force?

- What steps might you take to increase your credibility with the task force members?

- Given the individual characteristics and values of each individual, which members might embrace the change and which resist? What would you expect to be the bases of resistance? How would you strategize to overcome the resistance? What data and facts might be important to keep in front of the team to reduce resistance?

- What members of the team might ally with each other? What conflicts might arise between and among team members? How would you plan to manage these conflicts?

- Would any member of the team perhaps make a good champion? If so, who? What steps would you take to enlist that person as an ally?

- What role would you suggest for the provost, recognizing that she is expecting you to lead?

CHAPTER 8:
EFFECTIVE DECISION-MAKING

As many people—including myself—have learned the hard way, being a leader and making decisions means that others may not always stand up and cheer for you. Another hard lesson is that many decisions are made based on best judgment. There is often not a clear yes-or-no, either-this-or-that choice. Through hard-learned experience, I discovered early in my career that I was sometimes prone to allowing my own perceptions, biases, ego, and occasionally inflated sense of expertise to weigh too heavily in my decisions. Also, when the politics became threatening, I sometimes found myself foot dragging over a decision or going along to get along when I should have taken a more decisive stance. It's part of being human. But it's important to understand that decision-making is one of the most critical skill sets for success in leadership.

There are many pitfalls to effective decision-making:

- There is a natural tendency to want to postpone hard decisions.

- There is also a natural tendency to want to get to as simple a solution as possible as quickly as possible.

- Decisive people—especially those who are considered subject matter experts on a topic involved in the decision—sometimes jump to the decision that their training and experience tells them is the right one, while ignoring important facts, implications, and views of key stakeholders.

- It's true that there are times when decisions can be made with relatively few steps. For example, some decisions carry little risk for outcome or for people's reactions, such as should the reception be held on Tuesday or Thursday? Other decisions are pretty much binary—legal versus illegal; existential—we either do this or go out of business; or even a matter of life or death. These types of decisions don't require a committee or a lot of debate.

- Other decision-making processes, especially those involving complicated issues, multiple perspectives, and impactful outcomes, are rarely linear. Or at least they shouldn't be. As I gained experience in having to make decisions in these types of situations, I gravitated to a decision-tree approach. I also developed a checklist of some of the attributes that I consider to be important to the process of making a decision and to the decision itself:

  ○ The decision is consistent with legal, compliance-based, and ethical standards.

  ○ The decision is aligned with organizational priorities that were developed through cohesive, integrated strategic and tactical planning.

  ○ The decision-making process is transparent, evidence-based, and credible to stakeholders.

  Note: There are clearly rare occasions in which the process cannot be made fully transparent, such as when the confidentiality of an individual should not be compromised due to increased risk for that person or when sharing information contradicts legal protocol. However, in most circumstances providing stakeholders with the most credible facts available and helping them to comprehend the context of the issues as well as the process for decision-making enhances the likelihood of support for the decision.

○ The decision is supported by consistently applied and effective processes and policies. Inconsistencies in interpretation and application cause credibility to be damaged.

○ The decision and rationale are effectively communicated. Note that this communication may need to be made multiple times in a variety of ways in order to reach all of the workforce in a manner that they may best understand it. The communication process may also need to allow a forum for questions and answers. Finally, consider carefully who is the best person to communicate the decision and how it was determined. It may be the CEO, because that person holds ultimate accountability. But if it is a technical decision, it may be the person with the most credible scientific credentials.

○ The decision process provides for formulation of contingency plans should there be changes in facts, unanticipated results, or subsequent events that require a different approach. In some cases, these plans may need to include an exit strategy.

With these attributes as a base, here are the decision-tree steps that I have kept in mind as I pondered complicated issues. Every decision is different. Some decisions require careful consideration of all or most steps. In other situations, some steps become more tedious than helpful and needlessly delay the decision or they don't bring value to or alter the final decision. It's important not to get locked into paralysis by analysis. But having the steps handy as a reference has helped me to think through alternatives carefully and avoid rushing to judgment with inadequate preparation. The list is certainly not exclusive of other considerations, and I invite you to list other steps that you think are valuable.

- Explicitly define the issues. Frame the issues in language that is commonly understood (i.e., be careful to avoid confusing jargon or verbiage that is overly vulnerable to interpretation). Provide context without intentional bias, supported by credible facts.

- Is the decision binary? That is, would reasonable people agree that there are really only two choices? Note: In situations that have significant legal or ethical implications, it is important to seek the counsel of experts to assist with the decision. It is also important not to postpone the decision, allowing consequences to escalate, or to become overly compromising and run the risk of complicity.

- Does it involve legal/compliance risk, safety, or quality implications? These matters can sometimes be a bit nuanced and debatable; however, as with binary decisions, it's important to have appropriate counsel from experts and to err on the side of lowest risk.

- Are there significant public-relations consequences? Damage to image, brand, or credibility is very difficult to recover from.

- Does the matter have to be kept confidential for legitimate purposes, such as to protect an individual from risk of harm (e.g., whistleblower), to protect the legal rights of the organization, or because of legal and regulatory mandate (e.g., privacy regulations)?

- Are there organizational-governance or administration outcome parameters within which the decision must be made? In other words, do those in highest authority specify the process and require outcomes that are within a specific range? Examples of these parameters include mission-critical (e.g., must successfully launch a newly developed product in order to stay in business), financial (e.g., must achieve a return on investment of at least 20 percent), public relations (e.g., must increase consumer preference by 15 percent), and competitive outcomes (e.g., must move from a number-seven ranking to a top-three ranking). If so, how are the outcomes prioritized (i.e., does mission critical trump "financial?). Are there specifications about how and by whom the decision is to be communicated?

- Who needs to be involved? Who needs to be kept informed?

- What is the best credible evidence (set of facts) that will influence the decision? Who is the most credible individual or group to research and communicate this evidence? Who is the most credible individual or group to make recommendations based on this evidence?

- Is there likely to be a lack of consensus with regard to one or more of the following:

  - Priority (choosing one strategy over the others)

  - Resource allocation (who gains and who loses in the budget process)

  - Control (who manages the decisions and the resources)

  - Disparate impacts (one group gains and others lose)

- Impact to tribal values/biases (violates closely held beliefs)

- If so, and the impact of failure to achieve consensus is high, how will you manage the decision and mitigate the fallout?

• Who will support the decision? Who will push back? Is there a facilitator or champion who has broad credibility among the key groups and is able to promote consensus and support?

• What contingency plans need to be in place for change in facts, unintended results, or consequences?

- Revisiting facts

- Alternate plan

- Refining the original decision, the execution, or communication of the decision

- Additional efforts to build support

- Pull the plug

The consequences of poor decision-making can be career limiting. Key leadership components of making good decisions on complicated or controversial matters include seeking input from those with the best expertise, assuring that the forum for debate among those with expertise is open and safe for all participants, adhering to credible ground rules of the process, holding the members of the forum accountable for providing fact-based analysis and recommendations, obliging all participants to listen to each other with an open mind and biases held at bay, and requiring a commitment from the team to consensus building and to supporting the final decision. Having the discipline and fortitude to develop and support this type of team approach will provide a powerful platform for both good decision-making and stronger organizational trust in the decisions that are made. It doesn't guarantee that your decisions will go unchallenged or will be universally applauded, but it does provide a base of integrity that will serve you well when tough choices must be made and communicated.

Exercise

You are the plant manager for a manufacturing company that for thirty years has been based in a small city. It is a subsidiary of a publicly owned corporation, located in another city, that is governed by a board of directors and managed by a corporate president who is your boss. Your company has enjoyed growth and is greatly valued as a major employer and good corporate citizen by the community in which it is located. The company president requests that you make recommendations about a decision that must be made. Due to company growth, shortage of well-trained local candidates to address strategic manpower needs, and emerging competitive issues, the board of directors feels that the company must choose among three options:

1. The manufacturing company must move to a location with a larger candidate pool.

2. The corporation must add a new location, moving some of the existing manufacturing activities and staff from the current location to a new location.

3. The corporation must develop new strategies to mitigate the problems of staffing (e.g., use more robotics or use new tactics to attract potential employees from other locations) and competitive issues (e.g., stronger and broader marketing or innovations in product).

You are asked to make and justify your recommendations within three months. Using the attributes and as many of the decision-tree steps as you think advisable, describe your process for arriving at and communicating your recommendations.

CHAPTER 9:
THE ESSENCE OF LEADERSHIP

As my leadership experience matured through the years, I learned some personally difficult but very valuable lessons about the essence of leadership. The items that follow are my own personal beliefs. You may have others.

Credibility

Credibility takes a lot of time and effort to be earned, but it can be lost in an instant. There are many ways to lose others' respect. Putting yourself ahead of others, allowing monetary interests to overtake doing what is right, failing to show empathy and respect to others, not walking the talk. I'm sure you can think of many others. I've seen some promising careers crippled by self-inflicted damage to personal reputation.

Ego Control

Check your ego. It's easy sometimes to get caught up in your own internal narrative: your position, your authority over others, your compensation and perks, your public presence .... If you start bringing inflated views of yourself into the way you make decisions and develop workplace and public relationships, it can result in the loss of respect and confidence that others have for your leadership. You may find yourself increasingly isolated and unable to develop and sustain effective workforce teams. You may find that you are developing a staff that salutes you in your presence and avoids you or undermines you otherwise. This is a very difficult position for a leader to be in when challenging issues arise.

Share the Spotlight

Sometimes the leader needs to let someone else step into the spotlight. While the leader must ultimately remain accountable for the decisions and the goals of communication, it is often advisable to let someone with superior technical or subject matter knowledge speak to specific issues within that expertise. I'm sure you have seen situations in which a top leader insists on remaining the center of attention to emphasize a position of authority, only to muddle through key details. Even worse, the leader's subject matter expert may then have to walk back inaccuracies and clarify points the leader misconstrued. I have found that in dealing with situations involving technical or specific knowledge-based issues, a presentation was much better received when I simply introduced the broad topic and then turned it over to the subject matter expert to walk the audience through the details.

Let Subordinates Lead

Once you have assigned leadership of a matter to someone who accounts to you, don't undermine that person or the process by continuing to offer your own incongruent public commentary. I've found it effective to ask for private briefings from the person to whom I assigned leadership, in which we discuss any matters that I don't fully understand or am not completely comfortable with. This allowed us to make any necessary course adjustments and discuss any necessary, broader, group-communication adjustments. Then my delegate proceeded with leadership of the issue. If there was any challenge to the outcomes, I let the leader explain the rationale for them. And if there remained significant challenge to the outcome, I retained accountability.

Give Credit When It's Due

Give acknowledgment and credit to other leaders when it is due. First, it is the right thing to do. Second, it builds trust and loyalty. It also reinforces an important aspect of the organizational culture that encourages people to lead with confidence.

Don't Make It Complicated

Don't make it too complicated. I have to admit to a personal trait of sometimes making explanations to support my position overly verbose and complicated. In my desire to assure that others completely understand my views, I've sometimes unintentionally confused them or caused them to tune out. As an example, I was speaking to a group of community members years ago about how healthcare delivery was evolving and how these changes required modification in some services at their local hospital. I went through my slide presentation, replete with graphs and utilization formulas. No sooner had I completed my explanations than an elderly lady in the audience raised her hand and asked, "Why won't you reopen that service you just closed?" I must confess that I've had to relearn this lesson several times. Through the years, I've endeavored to acquire the discipline of thinking through what those receiving the information will find most important and provide it in a manner that they are most likely to relate to.

Keep Stakeholders Informed

If circumstances or facts change and information you have provided is no longer the most accurate, communicate this to those who are following your actions. There is no shame in changing viewpoints or decisions when the situation changes or better information becomes available. But it is important to keep your constituents aware of the basis for the changes.

Show Concern

When circumstances are affecting people and anxiety or grief result, they need to know that the leader cares for them and is concerned about their pain. Empathy, sympathy, and genuine concern for the welfare of those you lead are important leadership characteristics. An absence of these expressions, in word or in deed, sends the message to your team that you don't really care about them. In the face of adversity or crisis, they look to you for comfort and hope. It is important that your actions match your words. Statements of false hope are pretty transparent to the recipient. If you know and they sense that circumstances make it likely that bad news is coming, honesty combined with compassionate treatment is needed. I'm sure you have witnessed how well and also how badly various leaders have handled these communications. The results can either be inspiring or appalling, and they remain in people's memories for a long time. That is good reason to think about your approach to these situations, but the more important reason is that when people hurt, they need compassion and support.

Maintain Composure in a Crisis

In times of crisis, people need leaders to remain calm and thoughtful in their response. That is a tall order for most of us. In healthcare, we conduct lots of regular exercises so that we are organized in our thinking and leadership when crisis hit. We design our response processes and conducted incident response drills for fire, storms, mass casualties, nuclear or chemical exposures, epidemics and pandemics, active shooter situations, and other calamities so that we waste as little time and mental effort as possible should the real situation occur. Not every crisis allows leaders the luxury of having thought out and practiced the response. But the models we established still inform us in times of other adverse situations. Having an established and competent incident-command team at the ready and assuring reasonable preparations for likely incident-related challenges (logistics, facilities, coordinated response with other entities, communications, disruption of services, and so on), provides the basic structure that facilitates an organized and thoughtful response to emergent issues.

- Another key factor for optimal performance in a crisis is engaging in day-to-day behaviors that engender trust and confidence among the leadership team. Too often, we see top leaders allow their own perspectives (or wishful thinking) to distort or block reliable information or warnings that their leadership cohort provides. Or they shoot the messenger. If the organization's culture is one that has a track record for safe and open communication and reliable, fact-based decision-making among the leadership team, it is less likely that those who make decisions will fail to take action or go off on a tangent in responding to emergencies.

Admit Mistakes

You don't get it right every time. Sometimes, despite your best efforts, your decisions or actions may yield disappointing results. You are human. You have blind spots and personal biases. Choices are often not clear-cut. Assuming the results are not calamitous, I encourage you to consider a few responses. First, don't beat yourself up. It is much more useful to review what happened and take advantage of opportunities to learn from it. Second, if you haven't already formulated a correction plan, consider what can be done to remediate suboptimal results. Third, own up to your decision and to the results. Honestly communicating these with constituents, along with your remediation plans, usually will earn their respect and trust. Finally, consider this unhappy situation as another plank in your management-development infrastructure. No one becomes a top leader because they were right all the time. What you gain from learning experiences makes you a better leader.

Not All Leaders Are in the C-Suite

Keep in mind that people who are not in the high-profile positions can sometimes be the most effective leaders in certain situations. For many years, I had the privilege of working with Carmen Sherman, a lead supervisor in the environmental services (EVS) department of one of the hospitals for which I had responsibility. This hospital was in a community that was very angry about some decisions at the hospital that were made shortly before I arrived as the new CEO. There was also a resultant sense of anxiety and disenchantment among the hospital staff. I engaged with the board and management team to develop some strategies to mitigate the local animosity and staff malaise. As we executed those strategies, we achieved only slight success in moderating the concerns. While the audiences I met with appreciated the information I shared, they did not respond as I had hoped to my logic-based detailing of the rationale for the decisions. They were in an emotional frame of mind and I was unconsciously escalating their frustrations with dispassionate, fact-based presentations, hoping they would understand the rationale for the changes. Frankly, I felt that I was running out of ideas to change the dialogue. During my regular town hall discussions with hospital staff, I began to notice that Carmen frequently stepped up with rallying comments that challenged all of us to think and talk differently about the hospital and the role it had in the community. I had a growing awareness that others respected and responded well to her. Her message resonated with them. When she spoke, it was not about strategy or public relations messaging. It was about her pride in the hospital's mission and in the work that the hospital team did. I included her, as well as a few other like-minded hospital staff, as sitting members of the local hospital-advisory council I had just formed. This group included some of the most vocal critics from the community. Carmen's leadership, coupled with that of her hospital colleagues, complemented my efforts in nearly hand-in-glove fashion. I continued to share information about how the hospital was growing and moving forward with important new services (the fact-based discussion) and they spoke from the heart about the importance of the hospital and the hundreds of people who proudly made their livelihoods there (the heart-based discussion). Over time, our community advisory-group members began to transition from anger over the past to interest in and even to support for our hospital development strategies going forward. Along with this, our hospital staff culture developed in positive ways. We sustained that effort over the next twenty years. As operational and environmental challenges came our way from time to time, we were able to maintain trusting communications with those in the community.

Carmen's leadership didn't stop there. She did an exemplary job promoting her departmental team. Her team was made up of mostly entry-level staff members, great people who often had few formal work skills beyond the things they learned on the job. Through her personal engagement with her staff and her constant coaching and encouragement, Carmen assisted many members of her staff to acquire new knowledge and to advance in the organization to higher levels of competency, responsibility, and reward. She was our de facto internal university provost. Her team was consistently among the most engaged and highest-performing departments in the hospital. They took great pride in their work and had strong accountability for the results. And their leader consistently stepped back and let them take the credit that was well deserved.

Respond to Questions and Concerns Promptly

An excellent role model for this is Chris Van Gorder, FACHE, who is president and chief executive officer of Scripps Health in San Diego. Indeed, Chris is a model in so many ways. I encourage you to read about his inspired leadership in an article in the April 10, 2015, Leadership and Management section of *Becker's Hospital Review*, which details his commitment to educating and communicating with his constituencies. Chris is one of the most capable leaders I have been privileged to know. His role in healthcare is incredibly demanding, even on the best day. He is a recognized and sought-after leader on a variety of stages. Yet with all the demands on his time and attention, he personally makes the effort to respond promptly to all of the questions and concerns he receives. He demonstrates through his actions that he values and respects the issues of those who contact him.

Have the Courage of Your Convictions

Although it is sometimes painful, there are situations in which you must take a stand on principles. To refuse to go along with actions that push your personal-value boundaries or compromise the values you are trying to instill in the organization may risk consequences from those who are lobbying you to join their positions. These threats may be political, relational, financial, or personal. Choosing to give in to such pressure may at the time seem less unnerving than holding the moral high ground. But if the issues are serious enough, losing your credibility and your reputation can be much more debilitating to your career than the sting of short-term unpleasantness you must endure in order to adhere to your values.

I had the good fortune of working for a friend and mentor who modeled the courage of conviction. G. Richard Hastings (Rich) became president and chief executive officer of Saint Luke's Health System the year I joined the organization. I had known Rich before he hired me. He was a professor in my graduate degree program, and I learned a great deal about healthcare finance in the course he taught. Also, I served with Rich on the Missouri Hospital Association Board of Trustees and on various related committees. We vigorously debated with others many healthcare-policy issues of the day. I experienced him as a very friendly, very kind, and engaging person, but someone who didn't equivocate when he believed strongly about an issue. But it wasn't until I was directly working for him that I saw the full measure of Rich's fortitude in the face of opposition. He met issues head-on in spite of sometimes-formidable pressures. His courage became very important to me, both as an inspiration and as a source of personal support. As we worked together with others to build Saint Luke's Health System, adding several new hospitals and expanding services into new areas, I sometimes found myself on the firing line, facing strong local opposition to policy and practices we were standardizing across the system in the interest of improving quality. There were services that needed to change and sometimes people who had to either be rehabilitated or removed from their positions. These were not joyful experiences. On occasion, I had to contact Rich to let him know that the local politics might become more publicly rancorous. His response to me was consistent: if it's in the best interest of quality and safety of service to patients, you need to do what is right and I will support you. And he did.

Exercise

You are the top manager of an in-store retail company that employs a workforce of 250 people. Your company has a long and successful history, but over the past couple of years, sales are declining because of increasing consumer preferences to shop online. You have plans to develop an increased online platform for your products, but realistically it will take at least twelve months and more financial investment than your company can currently afford to make. Your business planning has led you to the conclusion that in order to compete in the marketplace, you will need to reduce the workforce and convert those salary dollars into technology investment.

- What are some of the actions you would put into your plan?

- What would be the approach and content of your communications?

CHAPTER 10:
GOVERNANCE

I reserved a chapter to isolate focus on governance leadership, because I think it sets the framework and cultural expectations for all of the organizational-leadership activities we've just reviewed. In its best-practice state, it is the platform and the catalyst that promotes the most important contributions an organization provides through its mission. It sets policy. It chooses leaders and holds them responsible to carry out its direction. It sets organizational vision. It holds itself accountable to shareholders, stakeholders, consumers, and the public for ethical behaviors and operations. It provides the framework and guidance for entities—whether religious, legal, academic, governmental, commercial, or volunteer—to accomplish their important work for society. Conversely, it is a sad fact that too many governing bodies fail to have the knowledge and discipline required to carry out this critical leadership role. Their required functions sometimes break down around narrow parochial points of view, short-term thinking, self-interest, political gamesmanship, and failure to do necessary hard work. When this happens, even if they don't fail entirely, they still don't succeed.

In my career, I had the privilege of serving on the boards of a number of organizations, mostly not-for-profits that had responsibility for operating in the best interest of public trust. In several cases, I was the board chairman. I also had the experience of advising boards of other organizations. I was fortunate to work with some excellent leaders, people whose leadership skills, dedication, and selflessness were exemplary. They were able to face very difficult challenges with integrity, objectivity, diligence, and fortitude. They led their organizations to positions of trust and respect. I have learned much from them, and I'm proud to share what I've learned with you.

We live in a world of ever-accelerating change and challenge. Just think of what was considered the latest technology as the twenty-first century arrived. Think of how retail was organized: malls, video stores, and in-store shopping. Think of how banking was done and how you received your primary medical care. Now think of how these products and transactions have evolved and are continuing to be transformed ever-more rapidly. Given the magnitude of the challenges the world faces, from climate change to pandemics to societal inequalities, it is reassuring to know that humans are capable of making amazing advances. Some advances are the result of commercial endeavors. Some stem from humanitarian efforts and societal pressure. Some are thrust forward through radical pioneering spirit. And interestingly, the lines of these catalytic forces are converging in many cases, resulting in unexpected collaborations. But in order to have advances that are guided by the right purposes, the right leadership, and the right accountability to the public they serve, good governance is fundamental. We can't have twenty-first-century advances with twentieth-century leadership approaches.

For organizations striving to understand that they need to achieve best practices in order to sustain their missions and thrive in a challenging environment, I'd like to recommend a book that I think provides a ground-breaking perspective on governance improvement. *Principles of Twenty-first Century Governance: Journey to High Performance Boards*, by Dr. Les Wallace, lays out principles that can guide governing bodies of organizations—whether large or small, seasoned or fledgling—into discussions that will stimulate governance improvement. It challenges board members to competency levels and performance expectations that are far more demanding than those based on traditional standards. It also sets high demands for overall board performance that successful organizations will have to achieve in order to sustain themselves and thrive. And very importantly, in an age in which public trust in so many traditional establishments and iconic organizations has eroded, these performance expectations can provide a way to regain the loyalty and respect of those whom the organization serves.

Based on my own experiences and observations through the years, I'd like to share some thoughts about elements that are important in developing and sustaining high performing governance.

Developing an Effective Board Culture

Board culture has everything to do with how well it achieves best governance practice. Too often, board membership is a product of social relationships or political aspirations rather than how each person's membership serves the best interests of the organization and those it serves. So how does an organization move forward with continual improvement?

Just as with development of the workplace culture, it is important to start with an objective analysis of how the organization is viewed by its consumers, its staff, and the community. Questions like the following can be helpful to begin the analysis.

- What do people who receive services or products from the organization think about its quality?

- How do employees respond if they are asked if it is a good place to work or if they recommend its services?

- What is its reputation for values and integrity?

- Is it viewed as a community asset and good community citizen?

This assessment demands an unflinching evaluation and effective plans for improvement in underperforming areas. It can also give guidance to the board in developing an objective matrix of selection criteria to be considered when filling vacant board positions, as well as in charting a course for developing a governing body that possesses key competencies, is representative of important constituencies, has relevant experience, and has the trust of the communities it serves. Each board candidate can be evaluated objectively against the criteria to ensure that selection to the board is accomplished with a process that keeps the interests of the organization and the consumer as its top priority.

Staying Focused on Mission, Strategy, and Performance

Another touchstone to evaluate the board's current state is how well it is adhering to and achieving its stated mission or purpose. It is all too easy for an organization to lose sight of its key reasons for existing and to go off chasing the latest passing trend or fad. There are myriad other distractions that can divert organizations from a keen focus on what's most important. For example, a trap that organizations are sometimes susceptible to is allowing more dominant members with narrow or self-serving interests to highjack the agenda, taking time and resources away from what is the most important board focus. I recommend that, at least annually, a key group that includes all board members, the executive and leadership teams, and key stakeholders and subject matter experts spend time conducting a meaningful analysis of environmental and operational risks, an employee-engagement assessment, and educational sessions on industry best practices and trends. These should guide the strategic planning-update process, which—though usually done annually—should have at least a three- to five-year horizon. Time on the board's agenda should reflect the key priorities stemming from the strategic plan, which should include the current mission and values priorities, along with meaningful review of performance indicators.

Disciplined management of the agenda does not necessarily exclude providing time to discuss emerging issues, it simply keeps the board focused on the most important matters for which it is accountable. It also reduces the risk of the agenda becoming sidetracked on non-productive or narrow individual-driven matters. I also recommend that the board conduct an annual performance review of its individual members. This might include a review of attendance at board meetings and other required events of participation. It might also include a board self-assessment, in which members rate the board's performance on the key priorities and provide their own assessment of how well prepared they feel individually to deal with the accountabilities of board membership. This can guide the board on development of an improvement plan.

Planning for Sustainability and Adaptability

The board and top management of the organization should not only be focused on the time horizon encompassed by the strategic plan. It should set aside time for regular education and for meaningful contemplation on how the organization will sustain its purpose and operations over the long term. It's very easy to get caught in the trap of thinking that the future will resemble the past and designing plans around that flaw in logic. Whether it is a technology upheaval (e.g., 5G competition driving the merger of competing communication technology companies), an environmental event (e.g., the COVID-19 pandemic), an innovation or market shift (e.g., Amazon, Uber, or Tesla), governmental policy upheaval (e.g., the Affordable Care Act, its implementation, and then efforts to disassemble it), or many other changes that challenge the traditional strengths of the organization and its products, it is an important function of governance to remain educated and aware. The board should hold itself and management accountable for plans to sustain the organization.

Board-Membership Requirements

Those seeking membership on a governing body should be prepared to commit to certain expectations in the interest of the organization's ability to sustain best practice. Each organization may have a somewhat different set of expectations. Here is a list of those I think are critical:

- Board members have a duty of loyalty to the organization. They should stringently avoid duplicity, undermining, inappropriate public comments, disclosing sensitive or confidential information, finger-pointing, or other forms of behavior that demean the organization. They should believe in the organization's mission and services, and in fact should choose to be a consumer of its services should the need arise.

- The actions of the board are the actions of the group, not the individual board member. There are occasions in which differences of opinion among board members will result in split votes. Members of the board may express their positions and can have their say during debate of the issue; however, the majority rules in the vote. In such circumstances, those on the minority side of the vote should refrain from behaviors and comments that betray trust in the board's actions.

- Board members should disclose and properly manage individual conflicts of interest and avoid giving even the appearance of self-dealing. Having a conflict of interest, in itself, does not reflect badly on the board member. In fact, it is a relatively common occurrence since board members are often very engaged in their communities. They or their family members may own enterprises that do business with the organization. They or their family members may serve on other boards that do business with the organization. They may own property that is the subject of negotiation with the organization. The list goes on. The duty of a board member with a potential conflict is to disclose it and follow the board's procedures in how to manage the conflict. Depending on the board's policies and individual circumstances, that may mean the person with the potential conflict could provide relevant information or may need to refrain from both comment and vote on the issue. The board chair, with advice of counsel if needed, should manage these issues with diligence and, of course, should adhere to these requirements in situations involving their own potential conflict.

- Board members have a duty to behave legally and ethically, not only in their roles with the organization but more broadly. Their behavior and decisions—good or bad, in the board role or in another activity—can reflect directly on the reputation of the organization they serve. Board members should have basic training in the laws and regulations to which the organization and its governance are held accountable. If there is any lack of clarity about an issue, the board has a duty to seek appropriate counsel for its actions.

- Board members have a duty to attend and to prepare for meetings by carefully studying materials provided, along with any other reasonable preparation that provides information and context for the meeting discussions.

- Members of the board should work to develop respectful and collaborative relationships with each other. This doesn't mean that they must agree with each other all the time. It means that they build a trusting relationship, learn how to communicate differences, and develop the skills required for problem resolution.

- The board should understand the difference in roles between itself and management. The board should exercise proper diligence in selecting a CEO or top manager, provide its direction and support to that person, monitor the manager's performance and give guidance where there is variance, and then let the manager lead the organization. When there is blurring of authority, it becomes confusing and sometimes disabling to others in the organization. It often results in mixed messages and unclear direction.

- The board should have a well-defined and documented process for filling vacancies. Best practice entails determining what characteristics best serve the requirements of the organization's purpose and performance, based on objective assessment. What skill sets are lacking? What constituencies are underrepresented? Are the diversity and generational mixes optimal for robust perspectives? Is the candidate a good fit in terms of personality and demeanor? Just as in the earlier discussion in chapter 5, those on the interview committee might do well to use behavioral-based interview methods in order to ascertain the candidate's ability to manage situational matters that may come under the board's purview.

- The board should commit to continuing education. The curriculum should be driven by the strategic plan, including the environmental and risk assessments. It should also focus on issues of innovation and long-term sustainability, including best practices of entities in other fields of endeavor.

- The board should commit to and participate in the afore-mentioned process of developing a culture of leadership by adopting and supporting policies on workforce behavioral expectations, taking the necessary training regarding crucial conversations and other organizational cultural skills, making the same commitment to behavioral covenants as others in the organization. (Note: The board's covenants may vary slightly from those of the employed staff, but should complement and reflect the same commitment to respect, integrity, and other behavioral principles.)

This list is not meant to be exclusive of other board best practices, but it addresses many of the issues that I have observed tripping up organizations and eroding their reputations. Board membership requires hard work and dedication to cause. It sometimes requires personal sacrifice. Service on the board requires embracing a fiduciary duty to assure to the best of one's ability that the organization is operating ethically and effectively, and that it is positioned well in the present to prosper in the future.

Exercise

You are a board member of a mid-sized, not-for-profit service organization in a community of 50,000. Your spouse is in an executive position and co-owner of a real estate group. The organization has on its board agenda a discussion involving the acquisition of some local property. The real estate brokerage service provider will be selected by competitive bid. What do you think would represent best practice as far as your involvement in the organization's selection process? Why?

- Participate in the board's discussion, because you don't really have enough facts to know whether or not you have a conflict of interest.

- Declare to the board that you have a potential conflict of interest, but still participate in the discussion because you have some measure of expertise based on your spouse's profession.

- Declare to the board that you have a potential conflict of interest and recuse yourself from further participation in that issue.

CHAPTER 11:
GROUP EXERCISES

For those who are interested in training as a group, let me suggest some exercises in which groups can be assigned roles. The following process works well.

- Describe the scenario involved in the exercise and the outcome you are seeking from the deliberations.

- Divide the participants into groups. (Note: Group size should be small enough to assure robust engagement of all group participants, and consideration should be given to whether you are encouraging heterogeneity of the participants in order to solicit diverse views or homogeneity to promote team thinking.) Require each group to have a scribe and a reporter (these can be the same person or different people).

- Assign each group a role to play in the scenario. Provide the group with pertinent information about the function of the role and description of the character occupying the role.

- Assign a time limit and ask the group to deliberate the situation, using the techniques described in earlier chapters of this book. For example, evaluating the likely points of view of other participants and determining which components of the decision tree need to be incorporated.

- When the deliberation period expires, ask the reporter from each group to discuss the findings of the group.

- When all groups have reported, engage all participants to discuss what they experienced and learned through the exercise.

Exercise 1: Star Rating Improvement

You are the vice president of consumer experience for a large service organization. The organization has four major regional competitors who provide essentially the same services as your organization. The market is very competitive, and profitability is highly volume dependent. The organization's marketing department has emphasized to management that the most significant driver of business is consumer ratings, as measured by a five-star program that is overseen by a national organization. The ratings metrics are based on the reliability of estimated versus actual cost to the consumer, service quality, service-provider professionalism, and overall consumer experience (e.g., convenience of appointments, on-time arrival, and communications). The number of stars awarded is an aggregate roll-up of the results of these individual measures. Your organization has received an aggregate score of three stars out of five for the past three quarters. Two of your competitors have consistently achieved four stars over this time period. The executive vice president of operations has charged you to form and lead a team to make recommendations to top management on how to achieve and maintain an aggregate score of at least four stars during the next calendar year. The organization's departments include: finance, human resources (which includes training), performance measurement and improvement, and marketing. Using the principles and techniques gleaned from the previous chapters, how would you proceed?

- Who would you appoint and what would be their expected accountabilities?

- What departmental values and biases would you anticipate?

- How would you structure the process in order to overcome anticipated conflicts between departments?

- To whom, how often, and how would you communicate the project status?

Exercise 2: A Question of Ethics

You are the chair of the board of a not-for-profit organization. The board is made up of eleven members and has a five-member executive committee. One of the larger donors to the organization's charitable foundation is a member of the board. You just received an anonymous contact from an outside source in the community expressing concern that a disreputable organization has enlisted this board member to encourage your organization to provide endorsement of its services in return for a large donation to the foundation. What should be your organization's response and how should you, as chairperson, develop it?

Exercise 3: The Well-Connected Board Member

You are the CEO of a not-for-profit service organization. One of the department managers of your organization came to you with a concern that a board member of the organization had exerted influence on him to change a product the manager's department uses to the brand sold by the board member's employer. This board member is also a member of the local city council, which oversees a portion of your organization's budget. What should you do, and what is the process you will use to arrive at a plan to address the concern?

Exercise 4: The Board Chair's Dilemma

You are the chair of the local school board. The board is made up of nine elected members. The district has a reputation for good performance. Due to state financial challenges, the budget allocation that the district will receive in the coming year will be dramatically reduced. This will cause a shortfall in the district's budget that requires decisions to be made within three months regarding which programs the district must reduce or eliminate. There is internal disagreement among board members and also between district administration and some of the board members over which programs should receive resource priority. Some of the board members are exerting pressure to terminate the district superintendent, who has previously had several years of high marks for performance. How would you organize a process for resolving these issues?

Exercise 5: Stuck in the Middle

You work for a large company that produces a variety of pharmaceutical and animal-health products. You were recently promoted from the position of director of data analytics to a newly created position of executive vice president of analytical research. Your previous training and experience are exclusively focused on data production and analysis. Your new role requires that you become part of the C-Suite team: the CEO and the executive vice presidents of operations, finance, product development, and marketing. The CEO has just given the team a directive that, based on recent instructions from the company's board of directors, the company must expand into a new product line to create novel genetic therapies. As you begin assembling a strategy to tackle your specialized part of this challenge—amassing artificial intelligence and existing evidence to create a base of knowledge for the company to pursue its research—you quickly run into some strategic and tribal conflicts with others in the C-Suite team. Some of the team members are pressing to skip steps to allow for quick production in order to be first to market. Others are concerned about existing resource allocations being reshuffled. Still others are not convinced that you really need all that research in order to be able to develop your recommendations. It shouldn't be that complex, should it? To complicate your plight further, some C-Suite team members are in conflict with each other over their own priorities and are pushing you to take sides. What strategies could you employ to begin to untangle these conflicts in order to proceed with accountability for your deliverables in this project?

CHAPTER 12:
BRINGING IT ALL TOGETHER—A PETITION FOR STRONG LEADERSHIP

I find it challenging to write this final chapter, because its premise reflects my personally held points of view, and these may unintentionally tread on yours. So, let me begin it by saying that I respect your right to disagree. We each have our own experiences that shape our personal assessments and opinions. I'm hoping that the ones I express lead more to consensus than polarity and to more constructive debate than argument.

We are living in very divisive times, not only in this country but around the world. But I would assert that we have more or less continually existed in divisive times. Focusing just on the history of the United States, the Revolutionary War left in its wake conflicting positions that the founding fathers took over the formation of our country. The Civil War was arguably the most epic example of divisive and destructive conflict in our history, and its residual disputes are still alive today. Following two World Wars and the Korean conflict, our country experienced generational conflict over the justification of the Viet Nam conflict. Modern-era civil rights conflicts are now in their eighth decade, with passions hot and solutions elusive. Current conflicts around cultural values such as globalism versus nationalism are churning politics. Societal inequalities continue to drive disparities in education, employment opportunities, wealth, health, life expectancy, crime, family situations, and many other facets of life. Conflicting points of view have become ever more eruptive, divisive, and polarizing. They have continued to degrade the values that many of us grew up with and previously thought were core to society: compassion, empathy, putting others before self, and seeking the greater good.

But I also assert that we now find ourselves in a period of acute national and global uncertainty, brought on by COVID-19, which offers the threat—or promise—of upending our views. It may change our perspectives on what we previously thought was really important and weaken the strength with which we cling to our past biases. It seems to me that this is one of those sentinel times in history that cries out for superlative leadership on many fronts: public health, the economy, rebuilding trust, strengthening science, tackling climate concerns, addressing issues of inequality, and many other imperatives. Our current situation spotlights our flaws in leadership and decision-making. Many of these flaws involve short-term thinking, legitimizing baseless claims, faulty prioritizing, embracing false narratives of binary choices instead of pursuing pragmatism and compromise, and placing politics over issue resolution. I'll leave it to you to interpret those comments according to your own viewpoint. The question is, will new leaders emerge that can break us out of these vulnerabilities? Perhaps some leaders were destined to greatness by the challenge of their times—Washington, Lincoln, Franklin Roosevelt, Kennedy, King—pick your own examples. But I think our greatest need today to meet both current and future challenges, is preparation to do great things. For most of us, leadership skills are developed, not a birthright. If you are on a leadership journey, I hope that sharing my own thoughts, experiences, and lessons learned will prompt you to probe more deeply into best practices, reach out more broadly to others with relevant experience, conduct more self-assessment, and commit to more self-improvement. And please contact me if I can help you along the way. We are in these challenging times together. Through your efforts to advance excellence in leadership, you're shaping my future as you shape your own.

ACKNOWLEDGMENTS

As you might imagine, trying to acknowledge the important counsel and support I have received over the many decades I have been on my leadership journey is a daunting task. The list of people who have influenced, encouraged, counseled, and supported me would consume nearly as much space as the text of the book. To those of you whom I include as a group rather than individually, please know that I remember and value each one of you.

Although I have had many opportunities to toss and turn at night over personally challenging management dilemmas, my exposure to the broad, real-life leadership challenges of my colleagues in healthcare has provided a much richer base of understanding, without which I would have had much less to offer in writing this book. In particular, I am indebted to those colleagues who have shared with me the struggles they encountered as they moved from their successful clinical careers to the unfamiliar environment of management. By helping me understand their individual challenges, frustrations, and fears, they broadened my own perspectives greatly. In the process, we forged strong confidences and friendships that I will forever treasure. I have refrained from including names in order to avoid breeching confidences, but I will forever appreciate our professional and personal bonds.

I am also grateful for the trust that other colleagues have put in me to talk through the worries and uncertainties they experienced as they sought the path for a management career or experienced career displacements. Through our shared experiences, I have been inspired over and over again by the power of collaboration in overcoming challenges. Additionally, I am so thankful for the mentors I have had in my career. The management world can sometimes be a very dark, worrisome place, and having guides available to light candles along the way made the difficult much more manageable.

I have been blessed as I explored and entered my post-retirement callings to have had the friendship and collaboration of colleagues who have helped me set a course. Lorie Eigles has helped me distill the universe of things I initially thought I might be interested in down to a focus on what I really wanted to accomplish and how I wished to spend my days. She continues to be a wonderful sounding board for my formative ideas. Tanja Heinen and Juliet Hawley, two former colleagues from my past, have re-emerged in my life as friends with whom I can share current professional experiences and receive valuable counsel on navigating the new challenges of becoming a published author. And I have had the great fortune of collaborating with Sherry Prindle, who works to expand my horizons based on the world of experience she has in developing and delivering innovative education and training on a national level, and from whom I obtained my certifications in professional and executive coaching.

I offer sincere gratitude to Carmen Sherman, Chris Van Gorder, and Rich Hastings for allowing me to share my personal stories about them. They are wonderful examples of what is right with leadership and with humanity.

I want to recognize and thank the thousands of people who are the heroes of the battle to overcome the pandemic tragedies that we are currently experiencing, those who put themselves on the front line at personal risk to deliver the essentials of our existence. There are countless examples of personal and team leadership happening every hour of every day. I salute each and every one of you.

Finally, I thank my wife, Linda. She has been by my side for the whole span of my career. Whenever I felt the urge to explore new challenges, she was there to provide support. Whenever I felt mired in worry, she was there to provide counsel and comfort. And whenever I needed someone to give me an objective and honest view of a speech I intended to give, a presentation I was going to make, or a position I had to defend, she has been there to provide it.

BIBLIOGRAPHY

Patterson, Kerry, Joseph Grenny, Ron McMillan, and Al Switzer. *Crucial Conversations: Tools for Talking When Stakes are High*. New York: McGraw-Hill, 2012.

Marx, David, J.D. *Outcome Engenuity-A Just Culture*. Center for Patient Safety https://www.centerforpatientsafety.org/david-marx/ *Accessed August 31, 2020*.

Abbajay, Mary. *Managing Up: How to Move Up, Win at Work, and Succeed with Any Type of Boss*. Hoboken, New Jersey: John Wiley & Sons, Inc, 2018.

Becker's Hospital Review. "Leadership and Management." "Chris Van Gorder runs a health system—and he'll never miss your email." April 10, 2015, https://www.beckershospitalreview.com/hospital-management-administration/chris-van-gorder-runs-a-3b-health-system-and-he-ll-never-miss-your-email.html *Accessed August 31, 2020.*

Becker's Hospital Review. "Leadership and Management." "Scripps' CEO Chris Van Gorder on the power of inbox-zero," https://www.beckershospitalreview.com/hospital-management-administration/scripps-ceo-chris-van-gorder-on-the-power-of-inbox-zero.html *Accessed August 31, 2020.*

Wallace, Les. *Principles of Twenty-first Century Governance: Journey to High Performance Boards*. Aurora, Colorado: Signature Resources Inc., 2013.